An Ornament a Day

25
Sparkling Holiday Trims To Make

Carol Field Dahlstrom

Brave Ink Press, Ankeny, Iowa

Author and Editor
Carol Field Dahlstrom

Book Design: Lyne Neymeyer
Photography: Pete Krumhardt
Illustrations: Shawn Drafahl
Copy Editing: Jan Temeyer and Jill Philby
Proofreading: Elizabeth Dahlstrom
Technical Assistant: Judy Bailey
Photostyling Assistant: Donna Chesnut
Location and Props: Roger Dahlstrom
Separation: Color FX, Peggy Card
Special thanks to those who helped execute
some of the projects in this book: Sue Banker,
Allison May, Elizabeth Dahlstrom, Alice Wetzel

ISBN 0-9679764-4-8
Library of Congress Control Number
2004092747

Copyright© Carol Field Dahlstrom, Inc. 2004

Printed in Mexico
First Edition

Carol Field Dahlstrom, Inc. and Brave Ink
Press strive to provide high quality products and
information that will make your life happier
and more beautiful. Please contact us with your
comments, questions, and suggestions, or to
inquire about purchasing books at
www.braveink.com or e-mail braveink@aol.com
or write to: Brave Ink Press P.O. Box 663
Ankeny, Iowa 50021

Look for other books by Carol Field Dahlstrom
from Brave Ink Press:
   Simply Christmas
   Christmas—Make it Sparkle
   Beautiful Christmas

About the Author
Carol Field Dahlstrom has written, edited, and
produced numerous crafts, decorating, holiday,
and children's books for 18 years. She has shared
her love of creating with audiences throughout
the country through speaking engagements and
television appearances.
Her products inspire
families to spend time
together creating,
learning, and celebrating.
She lives in the country
with her family where she
writes and designs from
her studio.

Symbols of the Season

Christmas ornaments are a symbol of the most wonderful time of the year. Every year as we carefully unwrap each trim, we smile as we remember Christmases past. And, as we add new ornaments to our tree, we anticipate new traditions and new friends.

Each day of December is filled with excitement as Christmas draws near. What better way to capture the excitement of that special month than to create a handmade ornament to celebrate each of those 25 days before Christmas? I know you'll enjoy using your talents to make these symbols of the season as you create An Ornament a Day.

Carol Field Dahlstrom

contents

Pastel pink and sparkling jewels combine to make this ornament a pretty addition to any Christmas tree.

What you need:
Purchased light pink matte finish ornament
Glass tumbler
Crafts glue with fine tip
Craft jewels or rhinestones in desired colors
Tweezers (optional)
Fine glitter

What you do:
Be sure ornament is clean and dry. Prop the ornament in the tumbler while you work. Work on one side at a time. Use glue with a fine tip to make a small starburst where desired on the ball. Add the jewel in the center using the tweezers. Dust with glitter. Continue until one side is finished. Let dry. Complete the other side in the same way. Allow ornament to dry.

This colorful clay mitten seems as cozy as the real thing.

What you need:

**Tracing paper; polymer clay in blue, yellow, and purple
Rolling pin; waxed paper; sharp knife
Small sieve; baking sheet; oven; crafts glue
Small paintbrush; purple glitter; 6-inch piece of cord**

What you do:

Trace patterns, *page 58,* onto tracing paper. Cut out. Roll all clay on waxed paper to a ⅛-inch thickness. Cut two mittens from blue, 18 circle shapes from yellow, and four jagged strips from purple. Cut one cuff strip from purple. Press yellow circle shapes on mittens. Press jagged strips on mittens to resemble stripes. Press front and back mitten pieces together at edges leaving top open. Wrap cuff strip at top of mitten. Push a ball of purple clay through sieve making strings of clay. Press onto cuff. Poke two holes at each side of mitten. Bake following manufacturer's directions. Cool. Brush cuffs and stripes with crafts glue; dust with glitter. Place the cord through holes to hang.

9

Five little evergreens group together to make this charming star.

What you need:

Five 3½-inch high bottlebrush trees (available at crafts and discount stores)

Hot glue gun; hot glue sticks

1½-inch diameter foam ball such as Styrofoam

Thirteen ½-inch diameter metal jingle bells

Red metallic chenille stem

What you do:

Remove tree bases by turning counterclockwise. Place a small amount of hot glue onto the bottom stem of a bottlebrush tree. Poke the stem into the foam ball and push until the stem is completely into the ball. Continue adding trees in this manner, placing each one next to the last to create a star shape. Glue jingle bells over the center of the star, covering the foam ball. Build up layers to add dimension, if desired. For the hanger, fold the chenille stem in half and loop around the end of one of the points of the star. Twist to secure.

SNOWFLAKE FEATHERS

Create these light and lovely snowflakes from delicate lace and pure white feathers.

What you need:

10 inch piece of white lace by-the-yard
(the patterns with pointed-edge designs work best)
Tacky white crafts glue
Clip clothespin
White feathers
White cording for hanging

What you do:

Gather lace in a circle by gluing folds to the center to make a round shape that lies flat. Glue edges together and secure with a clothespin until dry. Remove clothespin.

Glue the feathers behind the lace circle as desired. Slip a piece of cording through one of the holes of the lace or glue a piece of cording to the top of the ornament for hanging.

> **MAKE IT TOGETHER**
> *Prepare the lace and then let the children help glue on the feathers. Remember, just like snowflakes, no two will ever look alike.*

A familiar Christmas motif makes this frosty trim one that shines.

What you need:
Tracing paper
Pencil; scissors
Purchased frosted glass ornament
Dimensional paints in deep blue
Assorted glass paints
Paintbrush

What you do:

Trace the stars on *page 59* onto tracing paper and cut out. Lay the stars on the ornament, referring to the photo for placement ideas. Use a pencil to lightly trace around the stars. Using blue dimensional paint, draw the stars working on one side at a time. Let dry completely. Using the paintbrush, paint the center of each star a different color, using yellow, pink, purple, and blue glass paints. Allow to dry.

୬

Look under this fellow's hat to find some sweet little surprises.

What you need:
Large bell cup (usually found with stems attached in the floral section of crafts stores)
Drill and ⅛-inch drill bit
Air dry clay such as Crayola Model Magic
Acrylic paints in iridescent pale blue, orange, pink, and black
Paintbrush; pencil; crafts glue; white chenille stem
Purchased small black felt hat to fit bell cup

What you do:
Twist wire stem on bell cup; remove. Drill two holes ½-inch from rim on both sides of cup. Form a carrot shape nose from clay. Let dry. Paint bell cup pale blue. Paint nose orange. Let dry. Using patterns on *page 59*, draw a face using black paint. Paint cheeks pink. Let dry. Glue nose in place. Poke chenille stem through holes in cup; shape into a handle for hanging. Fill cup with wrapped candies. Place hat on snowman. ୬

ॐ

Simple white snowflakes and sparkling rhinestones make this ornament a wintry favorite.

What you need:
Purchased red ornament
Small towel
Small rhinestones in desired colors
Crafts glue
Toothpick
White fine-tip marker suitable for glass

What you do:
   Work on one side at a time. Rest the ornament on a small towel while working. With a pencil make five small marks around the top dividing the ball into five equal sections. Use a toothpick to make little dots of glue from the mark down to the bottom of the ornament. Place a rhinestone on each dot of glue. Allow to dry. Using the white fine-tip marker, and referring to the patterns on *page 63*, draw snowflakes on the ball between the rhinestone lines. Allow to dry. ॐ

Lines of paint, all swirled like the winter wind, intersect to make this elongated ornament a real beauty.

What you need:

Purchased elongated ornament
Glass paints in four desired colors
Small paintbrushes
White crafts glue
Fine glitter to match paints

MAKE IT TONIGHT
Suspend these ornaments by taping them to a shelf while working. Work on more than one at a time, and as one dries, continue to the other to make multiples fast.

What you do:

Starting at the top, make a swirl from the top hanger down to near the point. Continue making the swirls using only one color. Allow to dry. Starting with the second color, make swirls starting at the top, intersecting the first color. Allow to dry. Use the third color to make swirls, starting at the top, intersecting the first two colors. Paint the fourth color making swirls to intersect all colors. Allow to dry. Using a clean paintbrush, dip in diluted glue and brush randomly on the swirls. Dust with glitter.

FROSTED PINECONE

&

Dipped in wax and dusted with glitter, these ordinary pinecones become works of art.

What you need:
White candle wax; empty metal can
Old saucepan; hot plate or stove
Pinecone; wire
Pan or dish of cold water
Waxed paper; white glitter; ribbon

What you do:

Break up the wax and put in the empty can. Fill the saucepan about $\frac{1}{3}$ full of water. Put the can of wax in the saucepan. Heat the water. The wax will melt slowly. Never put the wax directly on the stove or in the microwave. Never leave it unattended. After the wax has melted, turn off the stove. Loop the wire around the pinecone. Dip it into the wax and then into the cold water. Dip it back and forth about five times until the pinecone is covered and white. Lay on waxed paper and immediately dust with glitter. Allow to dry. Tie ribbon around the top to hang.

POLISHED

Here is a good way to make use of those beautiful colors of nail polish that are collecting in your vanity—make a very polished Christmas ornament!

What you need:

Purchased clear glass ornament
Tumbler to hold ornament
Fingernail polish in desired colors
Flat glitter to match fingernail polish

MAKE IT TONIGHT
Because the nail polish dries so quickly, you can make multiples of these ornaments in just one evening and have a beautifully decorated tree to show your talents.

What you do:

Be sure the ornament is clean and dry. Place the ornament in the tumbler to keep it stable.

In a well-ventilated area, use the brush in the nail polish bottle to paint swirls and designs on the ornament working on one side at a time. Add more than one color of polish if desired. Sprinkle with glitter immediately. Let that side dry. Repeat for the other side. Allow to dry.

❧

Tiny rubber stamps and some gold ink decorate this pretty purple ornament.

What you need:
Purchased dark-colored ornament
Small towel
Small rubber stamp
Gold ink stamp pad
Ultra-fine gold glitter

What you do:
Be sure the ornament is clean and dry. Lay the ornament on the towel. Press the stamp into the gold stamp pad. Using a rolling motion, gently press the stamp onto the ornament. Repeat, working on one side at a time. Dust with glitter before the ink is dry. Allow to dry. Repeat for the other side. ❧

Decked out for the holidays in silver and pink, this pretty trim is made with markers and a dusting of glitter.

What you need:

Purchased dark pink matte-finish ornament
Glass tumbler; permanent silver marker
White crafts glue; paintbrush; fine silver glitter

What you do:

Starting at the top of the ornament, use the silver marker to draw two lines side by side from the top, underneath the ornament, and up to the top again. Let dry. Set the ornament in the tumbler with the largest pink area up. Draw a simple flower shape using the marker. Let dry. Turn the ornament over; draw on the other side. Let dry.

Turn the ornament upside down in the tumbler. Paint the glue on the area between the two lines around the ornament. Dust with glitter. Let dry. Remove from tumbler and touch up area around the hanger with glue and glitter. Allow to dry.

❧

This beautiful trim seems to echo the star of the first Christmas.

What you need:
Tracing paper
White polymer clay, such as Sculpey
Rolling tool or rolling pin; waxed paper; crafts knife
Objects to make texture in the clay such as
   toothpicks, buttons, screwdriver end, etc.
Baking sheet; gold metallic acrylic paint
Paintbrush; fine gold glitter; fine cording

What you do:
   Trace pattern on *page 60* onto tracing paper. Cut out. On waxed paper, roll out clay to ⅛-inch thickness. Place pattern on clay; cut out with crafts knife. Place on baking sheet. Add texture by gently pressing objects into the clay. Bring every other point to center; press to hold. Cover center with small ball of clay. Texturize center of ball. Make hole in top point. Bake following manufacturer's instructions; allow to cool. Paint with metallic paint. While paint is wet, dust with glitter; allow to dry. ❧

GOLDEN CONE BOUQUET

୶

Fill a golden paper cone with fresh roses for your holiday tree.

What you need:
Tracing paper; pencil
12-inch square of metallic gold cardstock; gold vellum
Decorative edge scissors; stapler; paper punch
6 inches of gold cording; crafts glue; gold glitter
Small roses; small water tubes

What you do:

Trace pattern on *page 61*. Cut out. Trace one pattern onto metallic gold cardstock and one on vellum. Cut out with decorative edge scissors. Overlap each cone to line indicated; staple. Punch two holes at each side of cardstock cone. Use crafts glue to run a bead of glue along edge of cardstock cone. Dust with glitter. Let dry. Tie a knot in one end of cording. With knot on outside of cone, thread cording through one hole and back through the other hole. Tie a knot at end to secure hanger. Slide the vellum cone inside the cardstock cone. Place roses in water tubes and place in cone. ୶

Pastel hues combine with a graphic pattern to make this contemporary trim.

What you need:
Purchased pastel yellow ornament
Small towel
Crafts glue in a bottle with a fine tip
Fine yellow glitter

What you do:
Place the ornament on the towel to keep it from rolling. Work on one side at a time. Starting at the top, make a fine line of glue from the top to the bottom of the ball. Add another line about 1 inch away from the first line. Connect these lines by adding horizontal lines between the vertical lines creating sqaures. Add small squares inside the larger squares. Dust with glitter while wet. Allow one side to dry before continuing to the other side. Repeat on the other side.

Bugle beads entwined with beads shaped like leaves make this trim almost organic.

What you need:
Elongated green ornament
Fine copper wire (24 gauge)
Bugle beads in greens and yellow
Leaf-shape beads (available at crafts stores and bead shops)

MAKE IT TONIGHT
Stringing the beads on the wire takes just a few minutes. Wrapping it around the ornament is even quicker. Plan on making at least six of these trims in an evening.

What you do:

Cut two 6-inch lengths of wire. Make a tiny loop on one end to keep the beads from falling off. String the bugle beads and the leaf beads in random order until the wire is nearly full. Loop the wire at the end to keep the beads from falling off. Starting at the top of the ornament, twist the top of one of the beaded wires around the top of the ornament to secure. Continue to twist the beaded wire around the ornament making a tighter twist at the end. Repeat with the second beaded wire. Adjust as necessary.

SNOWY TRIM

Melted wax and glitter combine to make this ornament seem like it has been in a gentle snow.

What you need:

Purchased purple ornament
White candle wax; empty metal can; old saucepan
Hot plate or stove; old spoon
Waxed paper
White glitter

What you do:

Break up the wax and put it in the empty can. Fill the saucepan about $\frac{1}{3}$ full of water. Put the can of wax in the saucepan. Heat the water. The wax will melt slowly. Never put the wax directly on the stove or in the microwave. Never leave it unattended. After the wax has melted, turn off the stove.

Hold the ornament over the waxed paper. Take a spoonful of the hot wax and drizzle it over the ornament. Add more wax until it looks like melting snow. Dust with white glitter while the wax is still warm. Allow to dry.

FANCY POINSETTIAS

Tiny Christmas-red stickers make this sweet trim so easy to make.

What you need:
Purchased matte-finish seafoam green round ornament
Small towel
Pencil
Purchased three-dimensional stickers
Crafts glue
Toothpick
Fine gold glitter (optional)

What you do:
Be sure the ornament is clean and dry. Lay the ornament on the towel to secure it. With the pencil, make a small dot where the stickers are to be placed. Place the stickers on the dots. If necessary, use a toothpick to add a dot of glue under the sticker to be sure it is secure. If desired, add sparkle to the center of the stickers by placing a dot of crafts glue in the center of the sticker and dusting with gold glitter. Allow to dry.

MAKE IT TOGETHER

Let the children pick out the 3-D stickers at the scrapbook store. Give each child their own ornament to decorate and with a fine-tipped marker, write their name and year at the top of the trim.

❧

Nature provides the perfect shape for this bright and shiny star.

What you need:
Starfish (available at crafts stores and shell stores)
Drill and 1¹⁄₁₆-inch drill bit
Pink acrylic paint
Paintbrush
Fine pink glitter to match paint
Fine cording

What you do:
Carefully drill a hole in the top of the starfish. Remove any dust from the hole. Use the paintbrush to paint the star pink dabbing the paint into the texture of the starfish as necessary. Dust with glitter while wet. Reopen the hole if necessary. Let dry. Put cording through the hole to hang. ❧

PLAYFUL PINWHEEL

❧

Create some holiday fun with a sparkling pinwheel ornament.

What you need:
Tracing paper; pencil; scissors
5-inch square *each* **of blue print and purple print**
    scrapbook paper
Spray adhesive; paper punch
Scrapbooking tile (available at scrapbooking stores)
Decorative brad; crafts glue; silver glitter; cording

What you do:

Trace pattern on *page 62*. Set aside. With wrong sides together, glue papers together and treat them as one. Lay pattern on top of paper. Cut along lines to center circle. Punch a hole in center. Punch a hole in every other corner of the paper. Bring the punched corners to the middle and line them up with the hole in the middle. Punch a hole in the tile; line up with other holes. Put brad through all holes and secure in back. Run a bead of glue around all paper edges and dust with glitter. Punch a hole in top of ornament and add cording to hang. ❧

Just as evergreens come in all shades of green, this pretty ball is covered with the lovely green colors of Christmas.

What you need:

Clear glass ornament
Small pieces of tissue paper in shades of green
Pinking shears
Decoupage medium
Paintbrush
Fine glitter

What you do:

Cut the tissue paper into small triangles using pinking shears. Working on small areas at a time, brush the decoupage medium on the glass ornament. Lay the tissue triangles onto the wet ornament overlapping the triangles as you work. Paint the decoupage medium over the shapes and continue in this manner until the entire ornament is covered. Add a dusting of fine iridescent glitter. Suspend the ball to dry.

Even if you can't paint a straight line, you'll love making this colorful holiday ornament.

What you need:
Purchased red matte-finish ornament
Glass paints in periwinkle blue
    and orange
Paintbrushes
Red glitter glue

MAKE IT TOGETHER
Let the children help paint these ornaments. The curlicues don't have to be perfect and the glitter glue is easy to use. The designs will be delightfully different each time.

What you do:

If possible, suspend the ball while working on it by looping a string through the hanger and securely taping to a shelf or ledge.

Starting at the top, use the blue paint to make lines that end up with a curlicue half way down the ornament. Let dry. Repeat using the orange paint. Let dry. Use glitter glue to make tiny dots on top of the lines. Allow to dry.

49

Shiny rhinestones wrap this simple yet stunning ornament.

What you need:
Purchased red teardrop ornament
White chalk or dressmakers pencil
Rhinestones in desired colors
Crafts glue
Toothpick

What you do:
Use the chalk or pencil to make dots starting at the top of the ornament and wrapping around to the bottom. The dots will all start at the top and then swirl down with equal distances between them. Add a dot of glue on the marks and place a rhinestone on the glue. Allow to dry.

PAINTED SURPRISE

A few drops of paint all swirled together make a beautiful surprise each time.

What you need:
Clear glass ornament
Transparent glass paints in
    desired colors
Glass tumbler; crafts glue; glitter

> MAKE IT TOGETHER
> *Mixing colors is so much fun and the results are foolproof. Let everyone in the family make his or her own ornament and then listen to the oohs and aahs.*

What you do:

Remove the top of the clear ornament. Choose three colors of paint that when blended make a pleasing color. Some examples that work well are: blue, red, white; green, yellow, blue; red, white, yellow; purple, pink, white. Pour in a drop of each color and swirl the ornament around. Let it sit in the tumbler for about 5 minutes. Tip the ornament another direction. The paint will take about an hour or more to dry. After the desired effect is achieved and the paint is dry, use crafts glue to make lines from the top of the ornament to about $\frac{1}{3}$ of the way down. Dust with glitter. Allow to dry.

JEWEL TONES

Swirls and dots of gold make this ball seem almost regal.

What you need:
Purchased dark red ornament
Small glass tumbler
**Metallic gold permanent marker (available at crafts
    and discount stores)**
White crafts glue
Fine gold glitter

What you do:
  Be sure the ornament is clean and dry. Place the
ornament in the tumbler to secure it while working.
Start at the top and draw swirls with the marker
coming about 1-inch down from the hanger. Add a
row of dots below this. Make more rows of swirls and
dots. Let dry. Add a drop of glue on top of each of
the gold dots. Dust with fine glitter.

ORNAMENT TIPS

Collecting and making ornaments for the holidays is one of the joys of Christmas. Here are some tips for hanging, packing, and storing these treasured trims.

HANGING ORNAMENTS

Don't limit yourself to hanging these treasures with regular ornament hangers. Try using patterned holiday ribbons, colorful clothespins, colored or metallic wire, chenille stems, raffia, or interesting yarn or fibers to hang your ornaments.

Depending on the theme of your Christmas tree, the hangers can add interest and sparkle to your holiday trims.

PACKING AND STORING ORNAMENTS

After the Christmas season is over, it is important to pack up the ornaments carefully so they will be ready for next year. There are wonderful premade containers designed specifically for storing ornaments. These are available at home centers and discount stores and are perfect for keeping your treasured trims in the best of shape. Because many ornaments are so fragile, individual compartments that come with these containers are ideal for packing these treasures away. However, there are other ways to pack these trims without spending extra money for these containers.

For the very smallest of ornaments, use egg cartons or even candy boxes. For bigger ornaments, choose plastic or sturdy cardboard boxes with flat lids that are not too deep and can hold one or two layers of ornaments.

Wrap fragile ornaments in tissue paper or small pieces of quilt batting. Stack ornaments with the heaviest trims on the bottom. Never stack over three layers of ornaments. Be sure lids fit snugly on the boxes and will not come off when being taken from a top shelf. Always remove the hooks or hangers from the trims before packing and store the hangers separately in a small box or envelope. Mark the contents of the boxes before putting them on the storage shelves.

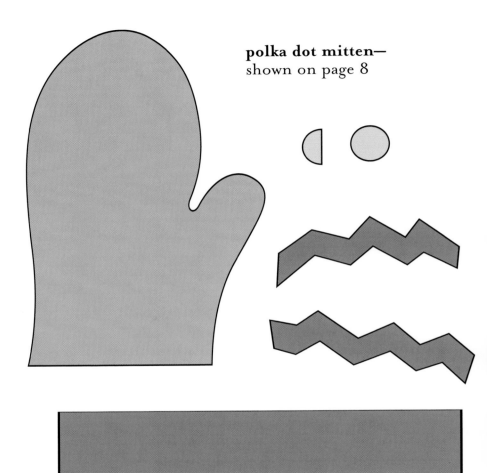

polka dot mitten—
shown on page 8

glistening stars—
shown on page 15

happy snowman face—
shown on page 16

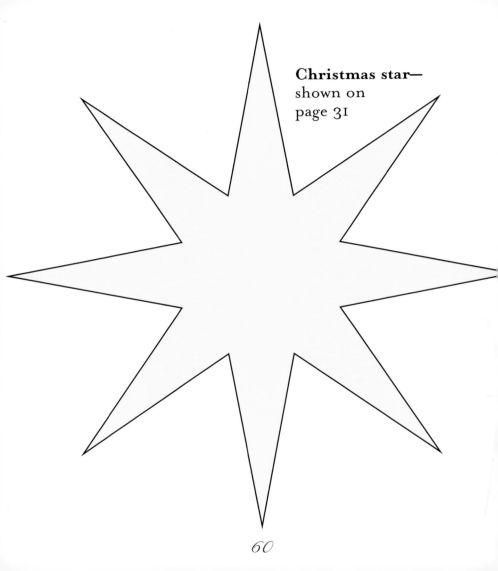

Christmas star—
shown on
page 31

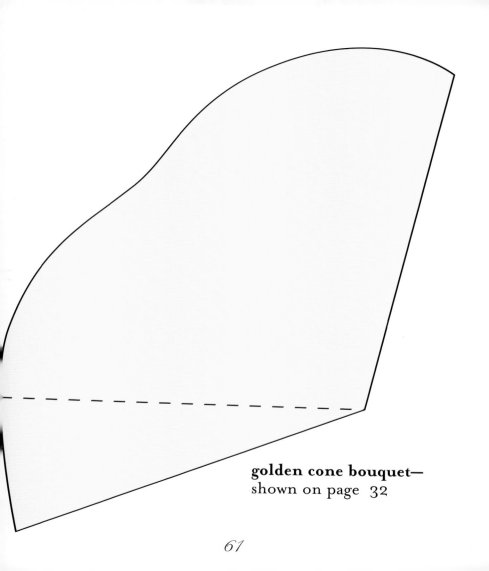

golden cone bouquet—
shown on page 32

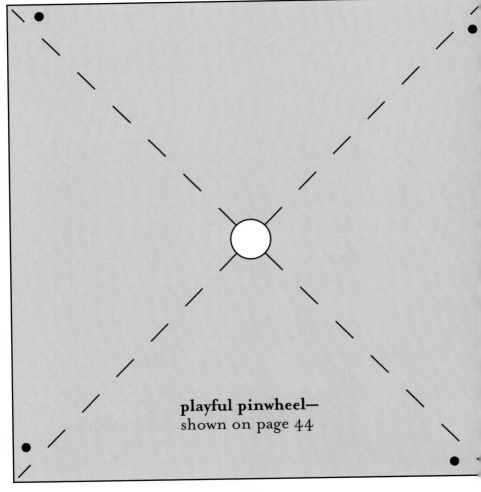

playful pinwheel—
shown on page 44

winter sparkles—
shown on page 19
(reduce to desired size)

ACKNOWLEDGEMENTS

೪

Lyne Neymeyer is a talented graphic artist as well as photographer and university instructor. Her exceptional understanding of design and her interest in pattern and detail have been evident in the beautiful books that she has designed for the past 24 years.

೪

Pete Krumhardt's photos can be seen in hundreds of magazines and books in this country and around the world. His creative use of lighting and his deep understanding of nature have earned him the highest reputation in the journalistic community.

೪

Special thanks to BJ Berti for her help and support in the creation of this book.

೪

This book is dedicated to Michael and Elizabeth who have decorated our holiday tree with their handmade ornaments for many years, making every Christmas one to remember.

೪